TO JON

REVERSE THE AGING PROCESS OF YOUR FACE

A SIMPLE TECHNIQUE THAT WORKS.

RACHEL PERRY

Printed in the United States of America

Published by
Rachel Perry Inc.
8137 Remmet Avenue
Canoga Park, CA 91304

Contents

Introduction

I am one of the many women in our society who grew up   7
believing (erroneously) that growing older meant losing my
looks, my sex appeal, my chances for a new career and success.
It has taken a long time to unlearn all of these falsehoods and I
am always continuing to learn, as I get older, that contrary to
my former beliefs, my looks keep improving, my sexuality is
not disappearing and I have more energy and creativity at my
fingertips than I have ever had in my life. I am involved in doing
things I love to do and feel better about myself than I ever have.

I was brought up in Hollywood, land of glamour and
youth, and became involved in a singing career at age twenty.
Between singing jobs I worked in Beverly Hills salons for a

woman who taught me how to give facials and do make-up work, using her own customized cosmetic line. My two careers have evolved side by side, and the learning process they have taken me through is what brings me to write this book.

Because I had to learn to overcome my own fears, plus the constant brainwashing of our society's youth cult, I had to prove to myself that I would not be "over the hill" by the time I was twenty-five or thirty. Since there was so much I wanted to do, and time was not standing still, I had to find a way to be ageless physically, emotionally and mentally. I sought out and found wonderful teachers from different parts of the world who taught me facial massage techniques, facial exercise and extensive skin care techniques. I also learned how to condition the rest of my body and mind with the use of good nutrition, dance, tennis, Yoga and meditation.

After experimenting successfully on myself, I decided to take the best of my findings and teach what I had learned to other people and see if they received the same great results. Rather than giving one person a facial, I started teaching a group of people how to do it themselves, every day. I kept perfecting and editing the technique so that it could become an automatic part of a person's daily routine. After all, what good is a technique if it is too drawn-out or complicated for a person to do every day? The outcome was fantastic. Everyone that used the technique started seeing results within the first month. At the same time, I had been developing a line of special nutritional skin care products to be used by my students while doing the technique. I didn't know at that time that these products would take off and receive such a strong following from ardent users all over the world. I found myself so busy getting my products out to the people, that I had no time left to teach my classes. I finally decided that the only way to share my technique, making it more available to more people, would be in the form of a book.

In the meanwhile, my music career had also changed its direction quite a bit. I had discovered a talent for songwriting that I never knew I had. My songs started to get recorded by major recording artists and, at the same time, I was also teaching these celebrities the valuable technique of preserving their youthful appearances. This only shows that there are no limitations on combining more than one form of creativity or more than one career.

I didn't learn any of these things overnight, but I did learn them because I was motivated to change the "neurotic destiny" I had thought was mine at a very early age. For this reason, I can tell you with *certainty*, that you too can change your so-called destiny, revitalize your entire being and Reverse The Aging Process of not only your Face, but your Mind and Body as well.

1

A SIMPLE TECHNIQUE THAT WORKS

14   I am going to begin this book by re-stating the title: **"RE-VERSE THE AGING PROCESS OF YOUR FACE:** A SIMPLE TECHNIQUE THAT WORKS!" It is this subtitle I now want to draw your attention to. Simplicity and effectiveness are the key. Being involved as I am in skin care, I read just about every new article and book on the subject. It almost always seems to me that the theories and techniques are long and drawn-out and many times too complicated for the average person to utilize. The bottom line is that there are a few very basic but vitally important steps to take in preserving and achieving a young, healthy skin, no matter what your particular skin type or age. Most of these books leave out the vital points and give a multitude of cosmetic recipes and superficial cleansing techniques that give a temporary new feeling to the skin, but no lasting benefits.

My sole purpose here is to give you a technique to last a lifetime and a book to read that you will not have to plow through to get the essential points.

In my experience teaching facial rejuvenation to both women and men, and in the time spent developing my skin care line, I found that there was a great deal of misinformation dealt out to the consumer, concerning the questions of skin massage and delicacy of the skin tissue. This has resulted in what I call *"The Overly Protective-No Benefit School of Skin Care!"* We have people approaching their faces with fear in their hearts; fear of stretching skin tissue, fear of irritating skin, fear of pulling muscles. Because of this confusion the facial muscles and skin tissue lose their elasticity and remain out of condition, just the same as out-of-condition body muscles. The premature-aging faces, of those who can afford it, are lined up in the plastic surgeon's office for face-lifts, ten, twenty, and sometimes thirty years before their time. And only because they didn't know some simple preventative methods to include in their daily routine.

I now want to give you a brand new point of view on the subject and a brand new skin to look forward to.

15

My approach for the past six years of teaching has resulted in great success for my students. It comprises a combination of Facial Exercise and Epidermabrasion (sloughing or massaging with friction), along with the application of scientifically designed skin care products. It does not consist of an endless series of complicated and time-consuming exercises that our fast lifestyle today does not permit. Once you learn the few simple Isometric facial positions, you can use them whenever you apply anything to your face, from cleanser to scrub, to toweling dry, to moisturizer, night creams and even make-up base. Herein lies the key. Each time you apply anything to your face, you will be automatically strengthening your facial muscles and rejuvenating your facial tissue. Think it sounds easy? It is.

The outer skin (epidermis) is shedding all the time, roughly a layer of skin a day, and there are about thirty layers in all. A new layer is being formed at the base of the skin every day. As the skin ages there is a normal slowing-down process of cellular reproduction. If the top shedding layers of skin are not removed, the growth process and formation of new skin tissue, to replace the old, is slowed down even more. This leaves the complexion tired and muddy-looking. The skin loses its youthful vitality and, in short, ages faster. But alas, don't give up hope, for by Epidermabrading the skin tissue and removing those top shedding layers you will now actually be speeding up the process of cellular replacement and reproduction. In other words, with your very own hands, you will be joyously reversing the aging process.

An interesting observation is that men rarely get the fine upper lip lines that are frequently present on a mature woman's face, due to the fact that they shave every day, automatically Epidermabrading that area and renewing the skin tissue. Some of the top dermatologists in the world are now agreeing that Epidermabrasion is an absolute must in achieving translucent, smooth skin. Excellent results are being obtained not only with the problems of dry and aging skin, but with overly oily skin prone to blackheads and even troubled skin prone to acne. The mechanics of Epidermabrasion aid in unblocking and loosening oily plugs in the pores. This allows the pores to be emptied of imbedded toxic matter more easily. Even if you have never before heard the word "Epidermabrasion," I am sure you will not soon forget it.

My technique is simply this: *You contract the muscle, hold it tense, and massage the area of the skin overlying it with friction.* You will strengthen and improve both the skin and the muscle this way. In the book "Face Culture"* by Dr. Frederick Rossiter, a specialist in facial anatomy, he says, "By contract-

17

---

*Frederick M. Rossiter, M.D., "Face Culture." Pageant Press Inc., New York, 1956 (Out of print)

ing the muscle, the skin is not stretched or loosened and it is safe to massage away wrinkles and encourage circulation at the same time."

Remember, circulation is the most important factor in having a young-looking face. It increases oxygen in the skin cells, carrying needed nutrients to the skin, and promotes the growth of healthy new skin cells. It also releases toxins that are lodged in the skin tissue, cleansing the blood close to the surface of the skin, which then allows the skin to breathe more freely.

I have seen, more than once in my life, ballet teachers getting on in age with the youngest-looking bodies and the oldest-looking faces. Why? Because they applied the basic principles of muscle rejuvenation to every part of their body except their face. It is this giant omission that I am endeavoring to correct.

You can now look forward to the years ahead, knowing that you can have a young-looking face at any age. I think that is a very exciting prospect, don't you?

2

THE TOOLS
YOU NEED
TO GET
STARTED

In the back of the book you will find a "STEP BY STEP   **21**
PRODUCT USAGE CHART." Use this chart as a guide to the
correct type of treatment product for your particular skin type
and the proper sequence in which to use each product; such as
1ST STEP—*CLEANSING CREAM* . . ., 2ND STEP—*ABRA-
SIVE FACIAL SCRUB,* etc.

I do advise the use of products that are pH Balanced[1], since
I feel they give the skin extra protection from deterioration and
premature aging. Many products which are not pH Balanced

---

[1]To be sure your products are the correct pH you can test them yourself. Simply buy SQUIBB NI-
TRAZINE PAPERS at your drugstore. Dip the paper into the product in question and compare to
the SQUIBB color chart provided. If it goes higher than 6.5, stay away!

are highly alkaline and tend to destroy the skin's protective barrier called its "Acid Mantle," thus causing it to lose its delicate moisture balance. In a young skin, this protective "Acid Mantle" is very prevalent and even after the use of alkaline products the skin bounces back to its normal, slightly acidic state in a very short time. But as the skin ages, it takes longer and longer to return to its slightly acidic healthy state. Products which are pH Balanced are designed to keep the skin in its healthiest state at all times.

22

You will start doing the *exercise positions and massage techniques* outlined in Chapter 3, using a good creamy cleanser for the 1ST STEP—*CLEANSING MASSAGE*. Follow this by toweling off cream using the same positions and movements.

The 2ND STEP is just a repeat of the 1ST STEP except this time, you will be using a good abrasive facial scrub in place of the creamy cleanser. Try to find a facial scrub made with as many natural ingredients as possible. These are most likely to be found in your local health food store. In my experience the two primary components that make for a great scrub are Sea Kelp and Sea Salt. They have a mildly abrasive action, are anti-bacterial and give a smooth, refined texture to the skin. If you cannot find a facial scrub that features these two elements as their major ingredients, then I suggest you buy a box of Sea Salt and some granulated Sea Kelp and mix some of each into the scrub you have purchased.

Since this technique involves Epidermabrasion, the first thing I will say is that you are the best judge of how abrasive to be with your own skin. If your skin is overly sensitive, dilute the scrub with water at first and as your skin adjusts to the abrasiveness, gradually increase the scrub-to-water ratio. A good scrub will draw impurities from the skin as well as remove dead, dry skin cells and stimulate healthy circulation.

You will get the most abrasive effect using it on a dry skin. So if your skin is not too sensitive, for the maximum benefit, be sure your face is dry before starting the scrub massage. Again, I repeat, let your skin tell you how it feels. As your skin texture gets stronger it will take more abrasiveness. *(It is this combination of Epidermabrasion with Muscle Toning that makes this technique work.)*

Follow the scrub with a toner or astringent (depending on your skin type), and then apply a good moisturizing cream or nourishing treatment cream. (See Chapter 6 on Moisturizing and Nourishment.)

Always remember to do the exercise positions and massage techniques every single time you apply cleanser, scrub, moisturizer, night cream, and even make-up base.

They will soon become totally automatic and you won't even have to think about them. You will notice your skin being more receptive to nourishing creams and obtaining a gorgeous, new, glowing, youthful look.

3

AND NOW
THE
EXERCISES

You will go through all of the following *exercise positions and massage techniques*[2] using the products as prescribed in each STEP of the Product Usage Chart for Facial Care (in back of book). The exceptions are the 3RD STEP Toner and Astringent, and the 4TH STEP Mask, which are applied rather than massaged into the skin.

27

EXERCISE ONE: This will keep the entire upper part of your face, including eye area, nose, mouth and cheeks, firm and uplifted and prevent and correct gradually sagging skin and muscles. Your skin tone will become increasingly more vital and glowing.

THE ETERNAL "O" *(See Fig. A)*

Exercise Position:

Form a large oval "O" with your mouth, pulling upper lip

---

[2]You might want to stand in front of a mirror at first while you are learning the positions (don't get scared—they will look rather strange). However, in a very short time you will know them by the way they feel rather than having to look every time you do them.

downward over teeth. Now without moving the mouth, smile, using the upper cheek muscles. At the same time squeeze eyelids tightly shut. There is now no loose skin tissue on face, and you may massage your face energetically without worrying about pulling or stretching the skin.

Massage Technique:

Holding the exercise position and using the fingertips of both hands, trace a complete circle around *eyes*, starting always from inner corner of eye, over eyebrows, to outer corners, then under eyes, including upper cheeks, completing a full circle. Do this about five times or to a slow count of ten.

Next, lightly massage *nose* with downward strokes (about five times).

While maintaining this position, again using fingertips, massage in a full circle around *mouth*, making five full circles in one direction and then five full circles in the opposite direction.

For *forehead*, simply place fingertips at bridge of nose, massaging upward and outward in long strokes to hairline (about five to ten strokes).

28

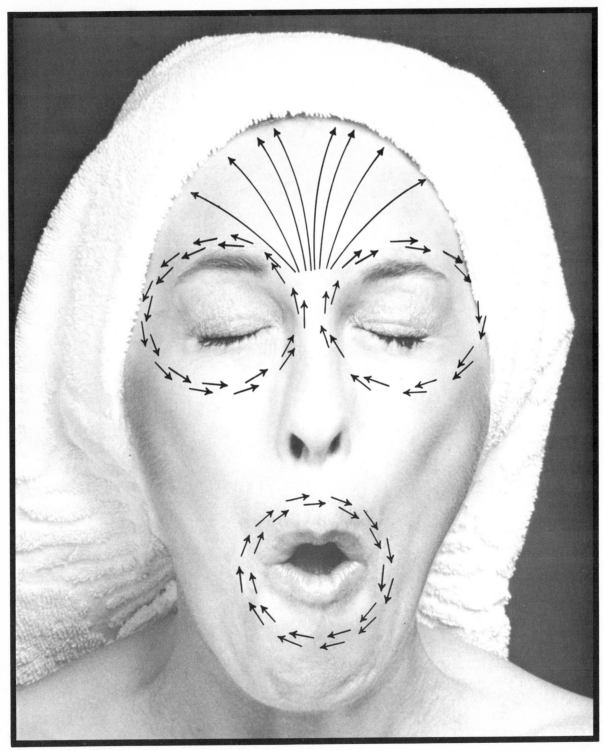

THE ETERNAL "O" (Fig. A)

EXERCISE TWO: This will keep the entire lower part of your face firm, preventing and correcting jowls and double chin problems.

THE FIRMING SMILE *(See Fig. B)*

Exercise Position:

For exercising the bottom half of face, roll lips inward over upper and lower teeth with about a half-inch of space between lips. Now smile as wide as you can with your lower jaw, as if your lower lip is smiling all the way to your ears. The rest of your face should remain unmoved.

Massage Technique:

Holding the exercise position, using the fingertips of both hands, massage the entire lower part of your face in small, outward, circular motions, starting at the tip of your chin, moving up to your ears and back down again, counting slowly to ten.

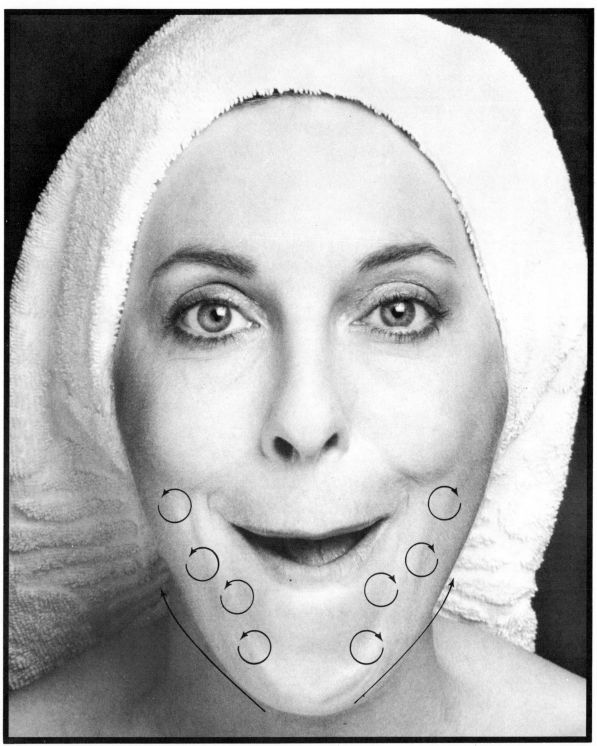

THE FIRMING SMILE (Fig. B)

<u>*EXERCISE THREE: This will keep the neck muscles firm and*</u>
<u>*the neck tissue smooth.*</u>

THE NECK REJUVENATOR *(See Fig. C)*

Exercise Position:

Place thumb directly under chin and curl the tongue back in the mouth until you feel the muscle directly under chin protrude. Now you may release thumb but keep tongue curled back in mouth. Now stretch your neck as far left as possible, with chin pointing upward, and slowly rotate to the opposite side.

Massage Technique:

Placing the fingers of both hands at the base of your neck, massage in vigorous, long upward strokes from base of neck to jawbone, while neck is moving in a half-circle arc from one side to the other. Do this to a slow count of ten.

32

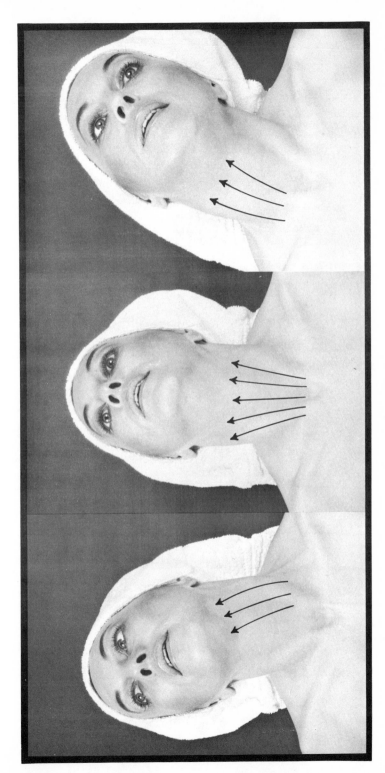

THE NECK REJUVENATOR (Fig. C)

EXERCISE FOUR: This exercise will do wonders for preventing and smoothing upper lip lines, smoothing furrows from mouth corners to the chin, strengthening muscles around the mouth and firming and filling out the lips.

THE UPPER LIP SMOOTHER AND AROUND THE MOUTH STRENGTHENER *(See Figs. D & E)*

Exercise Position & Massage Technique:

Press lips together in a straight line, smiling slightly. Count slowly to ten, massaging in tiny outward circular motions around the mouth, using the index fingers of both hands simultaneously.

Keep on squeezing lips together harder and harder until you feel a tingling sensation around the mouth muscles.

Now switch immediately to Fig. E. Make a small "O" with your mouth as if puckering up for a kiss and smile very slightly. Continue to pucker harder and harder, massaging in tiny outward circular motions around the mouth, counting again slowly to ten, then release.

Do this at least twice a day with the massage and whenever you can without the massage, such as when you are driving, cooking, cleaning, reading, etc. It will soon become automatic, easy and well worth the effort.

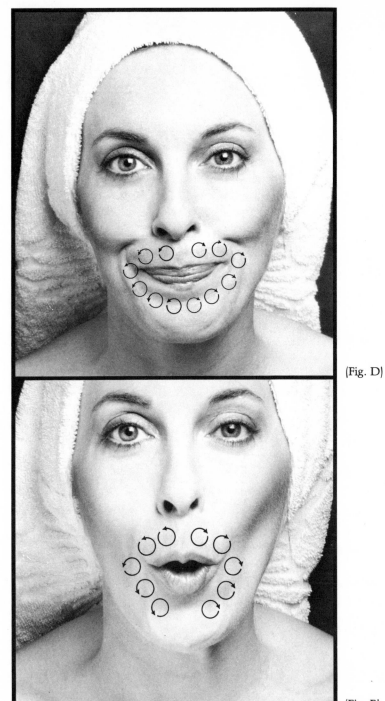

(Fig. D)

(Fig. E)

THE UPPER LIP SMOOTHER AND AROUND THE MOUTH STRENGTHENER

4

FACIAL
CLEANSING
—THE
WHOLE
STORY

CHAPTER FOUR

38

If you, as most of us, have read and utilized other skin care regimens before this one, you are aware that the first step is always a prescribed cleansing procedure. Lucky for you, you are now embarking on a technique where the cleansing procedure not only cleans your skin, but rejuvenates your skin tissue and the entire muscle structure of your face as well.

First of all, because you are cleansing as part of this technique your skin will become normalized and better balanced. For instance, if your skin is on the dry side, the circulation will stimulate the oil glands to work more efficiently. If it is on the oily side, the clogged pores will be unblocked and the excess oil drained and controlled, rather than running havoc with your face.

I have already instructed you to start this technique using a good pH Balanced cleansing cream for the 1ST STEP *CLEANSING & CLEANSING MASSAGE*. There are several on the market that are water-soluble, which means that they can be used with water as a face wash, if you have oily skin or if you just prefer washing your face for an initial cleansing. Remember, our 2ND STEP *(the SCRUB MASSAGE)* will give you a good rinsing-off anyway. For those of you who wear make-up, the cleansing cream should be used first to remove the make-up, then re-applied to start the 1ST STEP *CLEANSING MASSAGE*. In other words, in this case, the first application of cleansing cream is used before starting the actual technique. You wouldn't want to massage old make-up into your skin, would you? The same thing applies if your skin feels grimy or dirty; just give it a quick once-over lightly with the cleansing cream, remove the cream with a towel, washcloth or cotton, and then re-apply the cream and start the 1ST STEP *CLEANSING MASSAGE*. This will allow you to maintain excellent skin hygiene.

The toweling procedure is very important to understand. Get yourself an ample supply of small, rough white towels to last between laundry days. You can keep washing them over and over. I have enough to last me a week and every six days I throw all the dirty ones in the laundry and start over again. Set these towels aside as your special facial towels. At the end of the 1ST STEP *CLEANSING MASSAGE*, repeating the *exercise positions*, start with one end of the towel and as per the *massage technique*, use the towel this time, instead of your fingers. Then move to a clean part of the towel and do the next part of your face. For example, say your face is in "THE ETERNAL 'O'" Position. Start with your right eye and make a full circle around the eye with the towel. Then move to a clean piece of towel and proceed to the left eye. As you move through each area of your face, nose, around mouth, forehead, etc., keep moving the towel to a clean spot. One towel can go a long way since you can use both sides. By doing this you will not only get a good deal of circulation from the towel massage, but you will also know exactly how much dirt and grime are left on your face. When that white towel shows the remains of only cleansing cream, you will know your skin is clean, and you can go on to the 2ND STEP. If, however, there is still grime showing on the towel, re-apply the cream and towel-off once again.

The 2ND STEP *SCRUB MASSAGE* is the real deep pore cleansing. I never feel that my cleansing is complete until after I do my *SCRUB MASSAGE*. This is where the deep, stubborn impurities are drawn out and the dead, dry layers of skin are removed, leaving the skin like satin. Again you will repeat the proper *exercise positions and massage techniques* and you are now ready to rinse. My instruction here is to rinse with warm to very warm water. In fact, as close to hot as your particular skin can take comfortably (no burns, please). Rinse several times until the skin is totally clean. The warm water is wonderful for increasing the blood flow in the tissues, stimulating glands to work more efficiently (that goes for both oily and dry skin problems), loosening deep-seated toxins in the pores and generally enlivening the skin tone.

You may now apply a skin toner for dry skin or an astringent for oily skin. If you have a normal skin type (one that is not too dry or too oily) or a combination skin type (one that is oily in spots and dry in other spots) you may use either toner or astringent. This will encourage the pores to close again after your "grand opening pore cleansing." Be sure, however, that you find a toner or astringent that is pH Balanced. This is very important in order to put your skin into its proper and protected balance, as I discussed in Chapter 2.

I myself have not used soap on my face in many years. I do not like the feeling that soap leaves and since most cake soaps are highly alkaline in their pH and are certainly capable of stripping the skin of its protective Acid Mantle, I never go near them. However, if you are one of the people who cannot live without soap, there are some pH Balanced bar soaps such as the Redken Amino-Pon Cleansing Bar and others like it found mostly in health food stores. If you use a pH Balanced soap, use it between the 1ST STEP *CLEANSING MASSAGE*, and the 2ND STEP *SCRUB MASSAGE*. Do not use it to substitute any steps in the procedure, and apply it with the same *exercise positions and massage techniques* as in every other step.

After doing this daily cleansing procedure for a few weeks, the fresh new vitality of your skin will be enough reward to motivate you to make a habit of it.

5

THE
MAGIC OF
A GOOD
CLAY-BASED
MASK

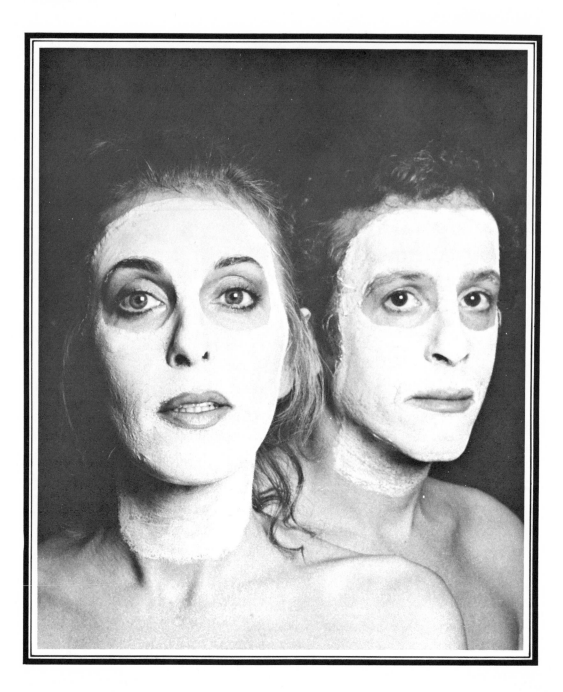

CHAPTER FIVE

It seems that I keep finding more and more uses for this   **45**
oldest of all skin treatments (discovered by the women of ancient Egypt while washing their clothes in the Nile River).

First of all, I am speaking of a good clay-based formula
rather than any peel-off type of mask. I fear that peel-off masks
can peel off more than dirt and grime. Possibly beauty marks
can be endangered and tiny hair follicles being pulled can cause
excess hair growth.

No such thing with a clay-based mask, however. Clay is a
totally benevolent healing substance that absorbs toxins, dissolves dead, dry skin cells, heals many skin irritations and
firms and tightens the skin tissue.

I have had the experience of getting up in the morning on the day I was to do a photographic session, having just gotten my menstrual period and when I looked in the mirror, I saw dark, swollen circles under my eyes. After going through my usual facial regimen, I applied the mask for twenty minutes and then rinsed it off. Lo and behold, the circles were gone. They just seemed to flatten out. This is the great absorbency power of the clay-based mask to reduce swollen skin tissues.

I have applied the clay mask to skin inflammations, burns and moisture rashes on my own body and found it totally soothing and healing, even when other remedies failed.

For the oily-skinned or acne-prone person, it is an absolute must in skin care, and should be used once or twice a day. At night it should be applied to any broken-out areas and kept on overnight. It will definitely help clear up break-outs and detoxify skin with no irritating effects at all. It will also minimize enlarged pores and help to refine a bumpy, coarse skin texture.

For the dry-skinned person it should be used two to three times a week as a stimulating, firming facial and to give a wonderful texture to the skin. Since clay absorbs dead, dry skin cells, there is an automatic renewal of skin tissue with each use.

Even for the body skin which I discuss in Chapter 7, there

are great benefits from this type of mask.

The use of a clay mask should be included in your plans for lifelong skin rejuvenation. Check the Product Usage Chart in back of the book for your skin type and when to use it, then go out and buy yourself a good clay-based mask and discover one of Mother Earth's great beauty gifts.

6

MOISTURIZING
AND
NOURISHMENT
FOR A
THIRSTY,
HUNGRY
SKIN

MOISTURIZING
AND
NOURISHMENT
FOR A
THIRSTY,
HUNGRY
SKIN

CHAPTER SIX

50   Now I know it sounds a bit strange to relate to your skin
as being thirsty and hungry but it happens to be a proven fact
among biochemists and dermatologists that, even though a
skin may be oily, it may still lack moisture and vice-versa.
Skin is overly oily because the sebaceous glands are active, but
this has nothing to do with the skin's ability to retain moisture. To explain it a bit further, the outer layer of the skin is
called the stratum corneum. It is five to fifteen layers deep and
is fed from within the body, but it does not retain much water,
especially as the skin ages. The younger the skin, the more
moisture this outer layer retains. So moisturizing creams are
very necessary to act on these outer layers. A good moistur-

izing cream or lotion will both prevent excessive evaporation of moisture from the surface of the skin and also add water to it. Special moisturizing agents in these creams, called humectants, increase the skin's ability to hold the water in, once they are applied. Since the moisturizing cream is designed to lock in, as well as add moisture, it works best when applied on a damp or just-washed face. This way you are utilizing the cream to its fullest extent, locking in a fresh supply of water.

Another way to increase the moisture content in your skin is by humidifying the air in your bedroom. This can be done very easily by the use of a steam humidifier or vaporizer or even a pan of water on a radiator. These will keep the air moist for hours and will even benefit your respiratory system. Since most of us spend winters in heated rooms and summers in air-conditioned rooms, both of which are severely drying climates, the humidifier is a real Godsend, giving you a moisturizing treatment while you sleep. I live in California where the air is always dry and have met actresses from England who said that when they started living here their once beautiful skin started to crinkle and dry out almost immediately. They found that this nighttime humidifying, along with the use of good creams, returned their skin back to a beautiful English complexion. I highly recommend this technique to all airline stewardesses. They spend most of their time in what could be the driest climate of all—the pressurized cabin of an aircraft. The air inside the airplane measures less than three percent humidity and dry skin is a constant problem. Whenever I fly I make intermittent trips to the lavatory to dampen my face with a wet paper towel and re-apply my moisturizing cream. If you do a lot of flying, this can be of great help. It's no fun arriving at your destination feeling like your face has been out in the Gobi Desert during a wind storm.

Another moisturizing hint from the famous beauty expert Toni DeMarco, author of "The California Way to Natural Beauty," is to apply your moisturizing or nourishing cream as you are about to step into your bath. The steam rising from the bath combined with the cream will lock a good supply of moisture into your skin for several hours. (This of course means that you do your facial cleansing procedure before stepping into the bath.)

Now, you ask, what is the difference between a moisturizing cream and a nourishing night cream? All creams are a combination of water and oil in an emulsion. The moisturizers are naturally more concentrated with water and the nourishing night creams are more concentrated toward replenishing lost oil, in addition to nourishing the skin with elements that aid in encouraging the growth of healthy new skin cells. As we get older, the skin benefits more and more from these nourishing treatments. The basic oil keeps the outer skin supple and soft. This continual lubrication is an absolute must. There has been much research done on which elements do the best job and there are now good creams on the market containing soluble proteins which have been broken down into a molecular structure similar to that of the skin, to enable good penetration. These help build healthy tissue. There are also excellent creams containing vitamins and herbs which have been proven to have excellent rejuvenating effects on the skin. Some of the best and most natural of these components are (1) Vitamin "E", (2) Collagen Protein, (3) Lecithin, (4) Aloe Vera, (5) Ginseng, (6) Panthenol (Vitamin "B-5"), and (6) Vitamins "A" and "D", which always go together. You may look in Chapter 12 of this book to find out what each one is known for and read about other nourishing elements. You can't go wrong using creams which contain these good natural substances to condition your skin. Experiment and see which combination does the most for you and which texture feels the best. If your skin is very dry, you might prefer a very rich cream or you might alternate with a lighter texture cream every other night or day. If your skin is on the oily side, a good moisturizer may

be enough, along with a richer cream for just the eye which tends to get dry sooner than the rest of the face. Many people have combination skin which is generally oily in some areas and dry in other areas. This should simply be dealt with by treating the oily areas as you would an oily skin and treating the dryer areas as you would a dry skin. See the Product Usage Chart in the back of the book for your skin type.

Another question that comes up is the difference between night creams and day creams. Mostly, cosmetic companies put out moisturizing creams for daytime use because of the drying elements in the air, that we discussed earlier, and because they are usually light-textured enough to wear under a make-up base. I personally do not feel the need to make this division of night and day, and see no reason not to use a nourishing night cream all day or a moisturizer at night. The skin needs both types of creams for complete care and unless a night cream is too heavy to wear under make-up or out in public because of the oily appearance, go ahead and use it. I believe in alternating skin creams so that the skin has all of its needs fulfilled. If I use a moisture cream in the day then I use a nourishing cream at night and vice-versa. Sometimes I use one nourishing cream during the day and another one with different ingredients at night. Basically I just keep alternating between three different creams, all of which offer different elements.

Whichever creams you use and whatever your skin type, the most important thing is to *remember always* to do your basic *exercise positions and massage techniques* when applying them. Once again I repeat that this is what makes the big difference between partial skin care and really rejuvenating your face and reversing the aging process.

7

DON'T
FORGET
YOUR
BODY SKIN!

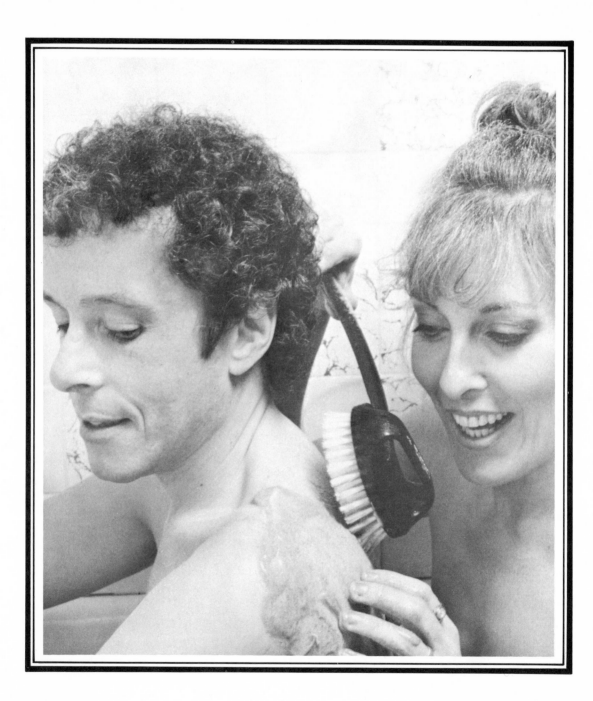

CHAPTER SEVEN

The same theory of Epidermabrasion (sloughing) applies   59
to your entire body skin. As with the face, go by your own skin
sensitivity. Get a back brush with a long handle (one that feels
comfortable) and every time you shower or bathe, massage
your entire body: legs, arms, elbows, back, chest; if you are a
woman encircle your breast area. Again, as your skin gets less
sensitive, buy a rougher brush. There is nothing wrong with
getting out of the shower after a vigorous massage, with a very
rosy body. It is just the blood coming to the skin's surface, rejuvenating all the skin tissue and giving all-over healthy circulation. It is also an important factor in helping to break down
cellulite. Cellulite, if you don't already know, is the name for

those not very pretty bulges and bumps that form in the fatty areas of some of our bodies and are basically an accumulation of trapped waste and water under the skin. It is a sign of poor circulation and possibly poor diet. It is usually dealt with in salons with methods of circulation improvement such as wrapping the body in warm flannel cloths to flush the system of waste materials, and also body massage and manipulation.

As far as I am concerned, Epidermabrasion (sloughing) and massaging the body should always be the other half of exercising the body muscles, just as we are doing with the face. After your dance or Yoga class or tennis game, or whatever your choice of body exercise, when you are ready to jump into that shower or bath, take that rough brush with you. And after the shower, towel dry with a nice rough towel. (Not the soft-velour type. They are pretty but do nothing for body circulation.)

I have developed a special body scrub[3] for this purpose, containing seeds and herbs that rejuvenate the entire body skin. It is used as a rubdown before the shower or bath on a dry

---

[3] "Spearmint Leaf Body Scrub"

skin, and as the grainy seeds are massaged into the body skin, dead, dry skin cells are sloughed off and removed and circulation is improved. It is then rinsed off in the shower and the skin is left satiny, invigorated and glowing. You can still use the rough brush all over before rinsing off the body scrub. It is hard to find these kinds of products on the market today, designed specifically for Epidermabrading the body skin, but they are there, and if you find one that looks interesting, by all means try it.

For an extra-oily body skin and possibly one that breaks out in areas like upper chest and back, a good tip is to apply a clay mask to the affected areas, after the scrubbing, showering and toweling dry. Leave the mask on overnight, every night, to absorb toxins and excess oil and it will surely help clear up the body skin. Clay masks are so good for so many things (see Chapter 5). For instance, body massage specialists are now using clay masks on the upper arms and thighs to help tighten, firm-up and re-establish skin tone after weight loss, also in conjunction with exercise. If this particularly applies to your case, I would suggest a body firm-up mask left on for 20 minutes two or three times a week.

I am definitely in favor of saunas, steam baths, mud baths and massages, all of which help circulation while relaxing mind and body. You can lead me to the nearest sauna or Jacuzzi any day. I love it.

Remember a very important point. After the body is Epidermabraded (scrubbed), steamed, bathed and toweled dry, it is in need of and more receptive to the benefits of a good body moisturizer. There are many good ones on the market. The best are pH Balanced and contain good skin nutrients (see Chapter 12). Massage your body from tip to toe and get ready for a new surge of radiant energy. It is your body saying "thank you."

8

THE SUN
...YOUR
FRIEND
OR FOE?

CHAPTER EIGHT

THE SUN
...YOUR
FRIEND
OR FOE?

The sun has so many wonderful benefits for our bodies and souls. Poems, paintings and songs have been created as homage to its glories. It warms us, gives us Vitamin "D" just by shining on us, and it makes us feel good all over.

But the sun's rays upon your skin, in anything but small doses, can have the most aging effect of any one element I can think of. Therefore, if you are serious about retarding the aging of your skin, you must take steps to protect your skin correctly from sun aging.

Let me explain simply that the protective or dark pigment of the skin is called melanin. This pigment absorbs the sun's ultraviolet rays. The process of tanning takes place when the melanin comes to the surface of the skin and this happens when the skin is exposed to the sun. In other words, melanin is the skin's protective mechanism against burning, and the *tan* is the way it manifests itself.

Now dark-skinned people have much more melanin in their skin than light-skinned people. Therefore, they can take more sun before the damaging effects take over, but dark skin will eventually still burn, become leathery and uneven in coloration as a result of too much sun. Fair-skinned people, especially blondes and redheads, have much less melanin in their skin and therefore have much less defense against the sun. One way of thinking about it is that you are born with a particular skin color and when you get a dark tan you are really changing the cellular structure of your skin. The texture thickens and becomes leathery and wrinkled and the natural elasticity starts to break down. Unlike the popular concept of the so-called ''healthy tan,'' it is actually a not-so-healthy thing to do to your skin.

On the other hand, I don't want to scare you away from all the pleasurable aspects of the sun, for if you are the outdoor type, there are many protective measures you can take to insure you against sun-damaged skin. First of all, if you play tennis, like I do, or go boating, hiking or a hundred other outdoor sports, get yourself a comfortable hat for sun shading. That is a start.

The most important thing you can do while you are in the sun is to use a suntan cream with a good sunscreen or sun block. Luckily, there are many good ones on the market today. The best ones contain PABA or Para-Amino-Benzoic Acid. It is part of the "B" Vitamin family and has the ability to absorb burning rays. It is a great natural sunscreen. Another natural tropical plant extract (See Chap. 12) is Aloe Vera Gel. Used for centuries, it is a wonderful anti-burn moisturizing agent and skin soother in case you do burn at all. I believe these two elements make a great sun-protection combo. You can use them in the form of a cream, oil or gel and/or combined with other ingredients. Whichever form you choose, use it before you go out in the sun, and always re-apply it after swimming no matter what the label says about lasting effects. After your day in the sun, be sure to apply a good moisturizer or nourishing cream to counteract the drying after-effects.

After reading this, I am sure you won't be foolish enough to get a sunburn, but if you know someone who does get one, my advice is to apply cool compresses to soothe and relieve pain and itching. No hot showers or baths, no friction to the skin, and after the initial burn calms down, apply a combination of Aloe Vera and Vitamin "E" in a lotion or cream form, to minimize peeling and keep the skin moisturized. Aloe Vera is one of the most miraculous healing agents for sunburn that I have ever experienced.

Be sure to tell the teenagers in your life that too much sun in the teens definitely leads to early wrinkles. Sorry to be such a party-pooper but a word to the wise should go a long way.

Anyway, I've always managed to have a great time on the beach, by the pool and enjoy all outdoor activities without any negative results, and I myself have medium-fair skin. For this reason, I consider the sun one of my good friends.

9

FOR THE
PREGNANT
WOMAN

CHAPTER NINE

Just a few words to you ladies in waiting to remind you   71
that while your body is in the process of changing its size, it is
vitally important to stay on this regimen of muscle toning and
circulation for the face and the body. The more consistent you
are while you are pregnant, the less of an overhaul you will
have to deal with after the stork arrives.

I am not going to go into the specific body exercises designed for the pregnant woman, as there are many good pro-
grams available from many sources. However, it is most important to do these exercises in conjunction with the Epidermabrasion technique described on these pages. This will increase the overall circulation and vitality of your entire body

skin, and will also help to alleviate the pain of aching and tired muscles.

A great tip to help prevent stretch marks from forming is this: Every single day, without fail, massage your tummy, hips and thighs with a good body moisturizer or cream containing Vitamin "E." I have seen the amazing results of this on friends of mine who followed my advice and achieved motherhood without a single trace of the nine-month stretching period. Vitamin "E" carries oxygen to the skin cells and keeps the skin pliant and elastic so there is not the usual fatty tissue breakdown.

In fact, after nine months of this nourishing skin treatment, your skin may well be as soft as your brand-new baby's!

10

ON
GROWING
A GREAT
HEAD
OF HAIR

I have discussed and elaborated on the benefits of Epidermabrasion for the facial skin and body skin. At this point I must inform you of the importance of Epidermabrading the scalp and its relation to growing a healthy head of hair, while eliminating abnormal hair loss and hair thinning.

There has been a good deal of scientific breakthrough in the mystique of hair growth and its opposite, hair loss, which was once thought of as being strictly hereditary. I am not saying that heredity does not affect the problem, but more and more ways are being found to counteract this particular condition. Lack of circulation, stress and nutritional deficiencies enter into the problem and when corrected become part of the solution.

As I have discussed, the shedding of dead skin cells goes on all over the body and this most definitely includes the scalp. The accumulation of dead skin cells remaining attached to the scalp can cause embedded sebum (oil) deposits, cutting off circulation and oxygen and therefore causing dandruff, hair loss and generally weakening the hair structure. In the case of dandruff, the dead cells clump together, attracting dust and bacteria, becoming large visible flakes, and obstructing the hair growth.

Stimulating and massaging the scalp will lift away the dead skin cells and scaly waste matter. It also encourages the flow of fresh blood to the roots, so vital to the cell renewal of the scalp's epidermis (outer skin surface).

Washing the hair frequently, every day or every other day, is the first important step to adhere to. I can already hear some of you with dry hair saying, "But that will make my hair even drier!" Quite the reverse. The extra circulation you will be giving the scalp with this shampoo/massage will stimulate the oil glands to work more efficiently to bring the natural oils to the hair shaft. If the ends of your hair are damaged or dried out, there are any number of wonderful conditioning shampoos, rinses and hair packs made with natural protein, vitamins and herbal extracts that can be used to renew and give body to the hair itself. These, however, are not a substitute for the basis of hair beauty, which is a super healthy scalp. So don't worry, washing the hair frequently will not dry out your hair, unless you are using an extremely harsh, alkaline shampoo. For those of you with oily hair, the frequent shampoo/massage will not make your hair overly oily, as some people say. Even though you are stimulating the oil glands, you are also keeping the scalp squeaky clean, free of scaly-oily waste material and therefore unclogging the choked hair follicles. The good old-fashioned vinegar rinse can help that excess oil problem.

By now, I think you are getting the message that regenerating the scalp and growing healthy hair consists of cleansing, stimulation and the great Epidermabrasion/massage. No matter how good your nutrition is, the nutrients cannot be carried to the scalp if there is poor circulation resulting in constricted blood vessels and an overly tight scalp.

I believe that a pre-shampoo massage, utilizing a mixture of a few very effective natural ingredients, is the key to solving ninety percent of scalp problems and increasing hair growth. My favorite combination consists of two plant extracts. One is

Jojoba Oil (see glossary), found in recent research by Dr. Javier Gomez to successfully remove embedded sebum deposits from around the hair follicle, to clean and unclog the follicle and allow relief from dandruff. This frees the scalp to promote renewed hair growth. The other ingredient is Rosemary Oil (see glossary), an herb known for its very stimulating, conditioning and antiseptic qualities. These two herbal oils can be found in health food stores or herb shops, and can even be combined with other herbal ingredients that benefit the scalp and hair. These two are the basics, however, and will work wonderfully for our purpose. In fact, I think so much of these two natural wonders, that I have developed my own scalp massage with a formula based on Jojoba and Rosemary Oils. To make your own basic formula, purchase the oils and simply mix one part Rosemary Oil with two parts Jojoba Oil and eight parts water (purified water if possible). Fill up any dispensing bottle, shake it up, and it's ready to use. Apply a moderate amount directly onto scalp. Now, using your fingertips, start massaging vigorously. Keep applying mixture until scalp is saturated and continue massage for three to five minutes. For maximum results this should be done while bending forward from the waist with head hanging down, to allow for blood circulation to the scalp. You will now be loosening up dandruff that has accumulated while getting rid of dead cells and debris. You will also be stimulating circulation, allowing the bloodstream to bring needed nutrients to the scalp, and of course you will be loosening up the scalp. Remember, a tight scalp grows little hair. After massaging for about five minutes, relax and leave the mixture on your scalp for another five to ten minutes, then shampoo your hair thoroughly with a good, gentle, pH Balanced shampoo. If you desire, finish up with a good pH Balanced conditioning/finishing rinse. The aroma of Rosemary Oil is quite pungent. However, don't let it scare you because the aroma does disappear from the scalp and hair after a thorough shampooing.

79

The frequency of this massage depends on your particular scalp and hair condition. If you are prone to dandruff and/or thinning or balding hair, or if you are intent on increasing your hair growth, you can do this pre-shampoo massage treatment daily. If your scalp and hair are already in good condition, two to three times a week may be sufficient to promote an even healthier, more luxurious mane.

You may also want to massage via brushing. This can be done after the fingertip massage, while the mixture is still on your scalp, or on the days you do not use the mixture at all. Brushing distributes the natural oils throughout the hair, removes accumulations of dust and pollutants, stimulates circulation and adds sheen to the hair. This again should be done by bending forward from the waist, head hanging down and brushing from back to front. Give it at least fifty to one hundred brush strokes. Some scalp specialists believe in using a natural bristle brush, while others feel that this type of tightly packed brush will pull at your hair and damage it. There is a Denman brush that I myself use, in which nylon bristles with rounded ends are set in a rubber pad. The bristles are set wide apart and therefore the hair cannot get tangled up in it. This type of brush glides through the hair and gives a great massage. All this brushing is best done either on dry or semi-dry hair in which our Jojoba-Rosemay Oil mixture can be easily brushed throughout. Never brush soaking wet hair, as the hair is quite elastic at that time and can be pulled and stretched to the breaking point. A large, wide-toothed comb is best for wet hair.

There is a condition of receding hair in women and children called Traction Alopecia. This occurs when hair is pulled too tight for too long, such as with pony tails or tight chignons, like those worn by dancers or models. Hair loss can occur at the hair line and be quite traumatic, so keep rubber bands out of the hair, or at least keep them very loose.

Wearing hats or wigs on a regular basis can also cut off the circulation and oxygen, endangering the scalp. If you do wear hats often, give your scalp some time off and a good vigorous massage in between wearings.

Last of all, for additional scalp circulation and relaxation, lie on a slantboard with your feet elevated, head down and spine straight, for about fifteen minutes a day. This is good for the entire body and really enlivens the complexion.

The Yoga headstand is great for sending the blood surging through the scalp, but if you cannot do that, the somewhat easier neckstand (found in any Yoga book) will do the job of increasing the circulation to the face and scalp, and Yoga experts claim it will also promote a healthy thyroid gland.

My main concern in this chapter has been to deal with the scalp, which is the absolute basis of healthy hair care and hair growth, rather than the styling of, or treatment of individual hair types. If you refer to the glossary at the back of this book, however, you will find my selection of proteins, vitamins and herbs such as Panthenol, Keratin, Henna, etc., that make up the very best shampoos, rinses, conditioning treatments and hair packs. I advise you to experiment with a variety of hair care preparations that contain these fine natural ingredients in order to find the ones that best suit your particular hair type. The largest selection of these natural products are found in your local health food store.

These are the fundamentals to great scalp and hair care. The results, of course, are in the practice.

82

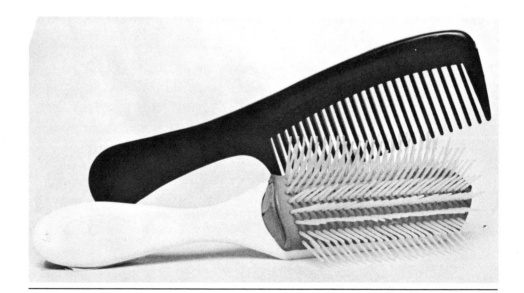

11

THE
ONCE-A-WEEK
SUPER
FACIAL

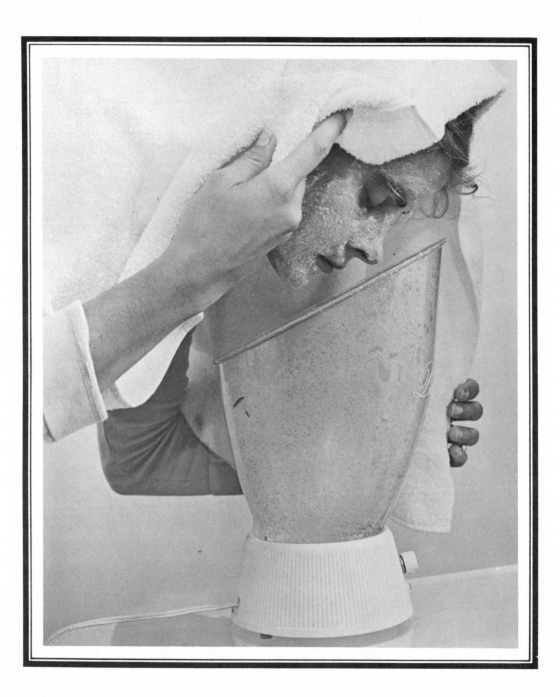

Now that you are getting the basic daily routine under your belt and hopefully it is becoming automatic, I am going to suggest a "Once-A-Week Special." It will give you a glorious feeling, you will look terrific and think you've been transported to a European facial salon. It is great to do before going out for a night on the town or on a Sunday night before starting a new work week.

First of all, start with your regular 1ST STEP *CLEANSING MASSAGE*. Towel-off and go on to the 2ND STEP *SCRUB MASSAGE*, of course doing each step with the correct *exercise position*. While the scrub is on your face, give yourself a five-minute facial steaming. You can do this with a small facial sauna machine, sold in department stores, or less expensive still, you can do it with a pot of boiling water and a towel to make a tent. Put the pot on a table and with a big bath towel, cover both your head and the pot, so that the steam rises up into your face. This will open the pores and allow the scrub to penetrate and cleanse more deeply. It will stimulate circulation and leave your skin rosy and radiant. But this is not the end. Now wash the scrub off with warm water and gently towel dry. You are ready for the next step—the clay-based mask. Apply the mask all over your face and neck (and if you wish to, areas of your body) and lie down for a good twenty-minute rest and relaxation period. If you like, put on some mellow music to help create a happy state of mind. Now, wash off the mask with warm water, towel dry, apply a skin toner or astringent for your skin type, let it dry naturally, and you are now ready for your last step—the *MOISTURING* and/or *NOURISHING MASSAGE.* If you are going out, apply a good moisturizer or a very light-textured nourishing cream and repeat, once again, your *exercise positions and massage techniques.* If you are home for the night, use your favorite nourishing cream and do your *exercise positions and massage techniques.*

This is your Super Facial and I think that you will like the exhilarating glow your face has taken on enough to give yourself this gift of beauty at least once a week.

12

GLOSSARY/MY
FAVORITES
FROM
NATURE

CHAPTER TWELVE

GLOSSARY/
MY FAVORITES
FROM
NATURE

The following is a compilation of ingredients most often found in "natural cosmetics" which are sold by and large in health food stores, and which I myself have experienced to be most beneficial when used in skin and hair preparations. Since many consumers are uneducated and somewhat confused as to what these words mean in terms of their personal use, I thought I would share some of my information with you. I have always found it very amazing that many of these natural substances have been used for thousands of years and have lasted through many cultures. Suddenly they are rediscovered and called a "fad," even though they have been around for centuries. I hope you enjoy reading about these natural substances and making your own "discoveries" and experiments into the wonders of nature.

ALOE VERA GEL: Comes from a cactus-type tropical plant that has been used as far back as ancient Egypt because of its extraordinary natural healing and moisturizing properties. The undiluted gel gives instant relief to burns and sunburns. It is a preferred component in many suntan preparations due to its wonderful soothing and protective qualities and its use is now being expanded to a variety of other cosmetic products.

ALLANTOIN: A derivative of the herb **COMFREY.** Used in cosmetics for soothing and smoothing the skin. Is known for its healing properties.

ALMOND MEAL: Used in grandma's time and still working for us, these crushed almonds are used in scrubs to cleanse, massage and remove dead, dry skin cells.

AMINO ACIDS: The chain of protein molecules that are the building blocks of the skin and hair. See **MILK PROTEIN, COLLAGEN PROTEIN,** and **KERATIN PROTEIN.**

APRICOT KERNAL SEEDS: From the pit of the apricot comes this wonderful scrubbing and cleansing agent that will remove dead skin tissue, stimulate and rejuvenate skin and draw out the impurities, leaving a glowing, silken finish to the skin. It is a wonderful abrasive treatment for sloughing the entire body skin.

CHAMOMILE: An herb used for centuries to condition the hair and skin. Gives hair a sheen, helps relieve inflammations of the skin and acts as an all-around external tonic.

CITRIC ACID: Derived from citrus fruits and used as a natural adjuster for pH Balanced products.

CITRUS OILS: From lemons, oranges, etc. Good cleansing agents. Also have an astringent, tightening effect on the skin.

CLAY: One of the greatest natural substances from the earth. It dissolves dead skin cells, absorbs impurities from the skin, helps reduce enlarged pores, firms up sagging skin and clears up skin eruptions. It has been shown to have great detoxifying and healing properties and has been used successfully for treating many different skin problems and inflammations.

COCOA BUTTER: Derived from the cocoa bean, it has been used for centuries in tropical and hot climates for its sun protection and lubrication of the skin.

COLLAGEN PROTEIN (SOLUBLE COLLAGEN): A form of protein that has been broken down into a molecular structure that absorbs well into the skin. Helps increase skin elasticity by strengthening the connective tissue that makes up our skin. Very helpful for dry, aging, or premature aging skin.

COMFREY: See **ALLANTOIN.**

EMOLLIENT: The term used for all lubricants which are soothing and softening to the skin. The richest creams have the highest quantity of emollients.

EUCALYPTUS: A tonic, cleansing herb that helps draw out impurities in the scalp and the skin. Is a mild skin stimulant.

GINSENG: The well-known Oriental herb acclaimed for its rejuvenating powers internally and externally. Helps stimulate blood circulation and healthy growth of skin tissue. Has a general renewing, stimulating tonic effect on the skin.

GLYCERIN: Another valuable substance used back in great-grandma's day for soapmaking and most cosmetic creams. It is derived mainly from vegetable fats and is used as a moisturizer and emollient.

GOLDEN SEAL: An herb used widely for its great detoxifying effects internally and externally. Works very well in facial masks and cleansing scrubs.

HENNA: Derived from the leaves of the Lawsonia plant grown in Persia, Egypt and Morocco, it was used as far back as Cleopatra and Nefertiti. The world's oldest natural hair coloring agent and conditioner is now making a comeback as the natural alternative to chemical hair dyes.

HONEY: Has wonderful healing properties and aids in drawing out impurities when used in scrubs and masks.

HUMECTANT: A special agent used in moisturizing creams, shown by research to draw moisture from the air and lock it into the skin to prevent dehydration. It is found naturally in Lecithin and Aloe Vera.

JOJOBA OIL: Used for centuries by the Apache and Mexican Indians as a scalp tonic, current research has shown that this waxy substance from the Jojoba Seed can remove embedded sebum deposits from around the hair follicle that cause dandruff, hair loss and weakening of the hair structure. When used as a scalp cleanser/massage, many people have claimed renewed hair growth, even in balding or excessive thinning conditions. New and varied uses for Jojoba Oil in cosmetics are being researched now.

KERATIN PROTEIN: One of the latest discoveries in reconditioning the hair. Keratin contains the same amino acid chain that makes up the structural protein of the hair. Because of this fact, Keratin has greater penetration into the hair shaft, and works on rebuilding and repairing damaged hair and split ends, as well as adding new body. Keratin combined with Panthenol make one of the most effective formulas when used in shampoos and conditioning rinses.

LECITHIN: Obtained from the soybean, this is one of the most important natural moisturizing agents because of its good compatability with the skin and its ability to penetrate into the skin. It is rich in Vitamin "F" (unsaturated fatty acids) and when used in creams, its emollient properties keep skin plumped up, soft, supple and youthful.

LEMON OIL: See **CITRUS OIL.**

MILK PROTEIN: A good source of amino acids and lactic acids. When used in creams and lotions, it helps to repair, smooth and strengthen skin tissue.

MINT: From mint leaves, it is used in facial masks and skin toners for its cooling, astringent, stimulating and anti-inflammatory effect on the skin.

95

OAKBARK: An astringent herb used as a tonic for skin and a highlighter for hair.

PABA (PARA-AMINO-BENZOIC ACID): Part of the Vitamin "B" Complex, this is a natural sunscreen that absorbs ultraviolet rays and protects the skin against sunburn. Works especially well when combined with **ALOE VERA** in suntan products.

PANTHENOL: A real wonder vitamin substance, also called d-Panthenol. It is a pro-vitamin "B5" of the Vitamin "B" Complex family. Lab tests have shown its great restorative properties for both hair and skin. When used in shampoos and rinses, it has been proven to thicken hair up to ten percent and help mend damaged hair. It has excellent skin absorption and has proved to be extremely healing and soothing for many kinds of skin disorders and irritations. It is an important addition to all cosmetics.

PAPAYA ENZYMES (PAPAIN): The extract of this tropical fruit was used by primitive Indian cultures for healing wounds. It effectively dissolves dead skin tissue and therefore is very beneficial when used in facial masks and scrubs.

pH BALANCE: The correct measurement of acidity and alkalinity in a cosmetic product, especially formulated to allow the skin and hair to maintain a slightly acidic protective film known as its ''Acid Mantle.'' To keep skin and hair in utmost health the pH should be between 5.5 and 7.0.

ROSE-HIPS: An astringent herb, rich in Vitamin ''C'' and a good addition to skin cleansers, toners, and scrubs.

ROSEMARY: A stimulating, tonic herb known to aid in hair growth, conditioning and scalp regeneration. It is one of the most effective components of any great scalp massage. This versatile herb can be mixed with any oil to make an excellent massage for aching muscles and to promote circulation.

ROYAL BEE JELLY: Direct from the queen bee, this substance is rich in vitamins, minerals and protein and is recognized as being an especially valuable skin nutrient and rejuvenator.

SEA KELP AND SEA SALT: Used separately or together in a scrub, these elements are highly effective for smoothing the skin texture, Epidermabrading, and regenerating the skin tissue. The Sea Kelp/Sea Salt combination makes for a great, mild abrasive. The anti-bacterial qualities of this combination help in the healing of skin eruptions by detoxifying and deep cleansing the skin.

VEGETABLE OILS (Unsaturated Oils): There is a long list of these beneficial raw oils: Apricot Kernal, Avocado, Almond, Coconut, Peach Kernal, Sunflower, Peanut, Safflower, Sesame, Olive Wheat Germ, etc., all rich in the unsaturated fatty acids, vitamins and minerals, so important for proper lubrication and nourishment of the skin tissue. They are used in the bases of many fine natural cosmetics.

VITAMINS: Used externally for skin:

"A": Helps promote growth of healthy epidermal cells and also smoothes dry and flaky skin.

"B": See **PABA** and **PANTHENOL** and **YEAST.**

"C": Research is being done now, showing evidence of improved functioning of skin capillaries and dispersing of small blood clots using Vitamin "C" externally.

98   "D": The Sunshine Vitamin. Has skin-healing properties and can be absorbed also by the skin through exposure to the sun. (NOT TOO MUCH SUN, THOUGH! Nothing ages skin faster than too much sun.)

"E": By increasing the amount of oxygen in the skin cells, this vitamin promotes the growth of new, healthy tissue. It also promotes faster healing of burns, minimizing scar tissue. One of the most nourishing properties for the skin, it aids in holding back skin deterioration and early aging. Also beneficial in preventing stretch marks when used during pregnancy or weight changes.

"F": See **VEGETABLE OILS** and **LECITHIN.**

YEAST: Loaded with "B" Vitamins and **PROTEIN**, this food substance has a very stimulating effect when used in facial masks. Induces blood circulation in skin tissue when used topically.

Charts

Step-by-Step
Product Usage Chart
for Facial Care

	1ST STEP	2ND STEP	3RD STEP
	Cleansing & Cleansing Massage	Epidermabrasion/Scrub Massage	Toning and Balancing
Normal skin	**Cleansing Cream** Follow with towel massage (Every day)	**Abrasive Facial Scrub** (Every day)	**Skin Toner or Astringent** (Every day)
Dry or dry and aging skin	**Cleansing Cream** Follow with towel massage (Every day)	**Abrasive Facial Scrub** (Every day)	**Skin Toner** (Every day)
Oily skin or skin that tends to break out	**Cleansing Cream** Use with water Rinse off and follow with towel massage (Twice daily)	**Abrasive Facial Scrub** (Twice daily)	**Astringent** (Two or three times dail or whenever skin feels oily
Sensitive skin	**Cleansing Cream** Dilute with water Rinse off (Every day)	**Abrasive Facial Scrub** Add water to lessen abrasiveness (Every other day till skin becomes less sensitive)	**Skin Toner** (Every day)
Combination skin	**Cleansing Cream** Use with water Rinse off and follow with towel massage (Every day)	**Abrasive Facial Scrub** (Every day)	**Astringent** (Once or twice daily)
CORRESPONDING RACHEL PERRY PRODUCTS	**CITRUS CLEANSER FACE WASH**	**SEA KELP-HERBAL FACIAL SCRUB**	**VIOLET-ROSE SKIN TONER or LEMON-MI ASTRINGENT**

Use this chart as a guide to the correct type of treatment product for your particular skin type and the proper sequence in which to use each product.

4TH STEP	5TH STEP	6TH STEP	7TH STEP
Firming, Texturizing and Detoxifying Skin	Moisturizing Massage	Nourishing Massage **Treatment A**	Nourishing Massage **Treatment B**
Clay-Based Mask (3 times a week)	**Moisture Cream** (Every day)	**Nourishing Treatment Cream*** (Alternate nightly with Treatment B)	**Nourishing Treatment Cream*** (Alternate nightly with Treatment A)
Clay-Based Mask (Twice a week)	**Moisture Cream** (Re-apply twice daily)	**Nourishing Treatment Cream*** (Alternate nightly with Treatment B)	**Nourishing Treatment Cream*** (Alternate nightly with Treatment A)
Clay-Based Mask Leave on affected areas overnight to help clear up breakouts (Every day)	**Moisture Cream** Massage on to skin while still wet from astringent and let dry (Every day)	**Nourishing Treatment Cream*** After massage blot off all excess cream except around eyes (Alternate nightly with Treatment B)	**Nourishing Treatment Cream*** After massage blot off all excess cream except around eyes (Alternate nightly with Treatment A)
Clay-Based Mask (Once a week)	**Moisture Cream** (Every day)	**Nourishing Treatment Cream*** (Alternate nightly with Treatment B)	**Nourishing Treatment Cream*** (Alternate nightly with Treatment A)
Clay-Based Mask (Every other day)	**Moisture Cream** After massage leave on around eyes and dry areas only—blot off excess (Every day)	**Nourishing Treatment Cream*** Blot off all excess cream except for dry areas (Alternate nightly with Treatment B)	**Nourishing Treatment Cream*** Blot off all excess cream except for dry areas (Alternate nightly with Treatment A)
LAY & GINSENG EXTURIZING MASK	**LECITHIN MOISTURE RETENTION CREAM**	**HI-POTENCY E CELLULAR TREATMENT**	**GINSENG-COLLAGEN WRINKLE TREATMENT**

*Use two different formulations for total SKIN NOURISHMENT.

Step-by-Step Product Usage Chart for Body Care

	1ST STEP	2ND STEP	3RD STEP
	Body Epidermabrasion Massage	Showering or Bathing	Body Moisturizing Massage
Normal skin	**Body Scrub/ Sloughing Treatment** Massage vigorously (Every day)	**pH Balanced Soap, Shower or Bath Gel** Follow with towel massage (Every day)	**Body Moisturizer** (Every day)
Dry or dry and aging skin	**Body Scrub/ Sloughing Treatment** Massage vigorously (Every day)	**pH Balanced Soap, Shower or Bath Gel** Follow with towel massage (Every day)	**Body Moisturizer** (Every day)
Oily skin or skin that tends to break out	**Body Scrub/ Sloughing Treatment** Massage vigorously Apply Clay Mask to any affected areas overnight (Every day)	**pH Balanced Soap, Shower or Bath Gel** Follow with towel massage (Every day)	**Body Moisturizer** (Every day)
Sensitive skin	**Body Scrub/ Sloughing Treatment** Massage gently (Every other day)	**pH Balanced Soap, Shower or Bath Gel** Follow with towel massage (Every day)	**Body Moisturizer** (Every day)
Combination skin	**Body Scrub/ Sloughing Treatment** Massage vigorously (Every day)	**pH Balanced Soap, Shower or Bath Gel** Follow with towel massage (Every day)	**Body Moisturizer** (Every day)
CORRESPONDING RACHEL PERRY PRODUCTS	**SPEARMINT LEAF BODY SCRUB**	**ALOE VERA ALL OVER BODY WASH**	**ALOE "E" ALL OVER MOISTURE LOTION**

Special
Sun
Reminder

		Special Sun Reminder for all outdoor activities
Normal skin		**Cream or Lotion with good Sunscreen** Use before, after and during all outdoor activities Do not bake
Dry or dry and aging skin		**Cream or Lotion with good Sunscreen or Sun block** Use before, after and during all outdoor activities Very little direct exposure Wear hat
Oily skin or skin that tends to break out		**Cream or Lotion with good Sunscreen** Use before, after and during all outdoor activities Don't overdo
Sensitive skin		**Cream or Lotion with good Sunscreen or Sun block** Use before, after and during all outdoor activities No direct exposure if fair skin
Combination skin		**Cream or Lotion with good Sunscreen** Use before, after and during all outdoor activities Do not bake
CORRESPONDING RACHEL PERRY PRODUCTS		**ALOE-PABA TANNING FORMULA**

CREDITS

JULIE FINGER
Design/Typography

ALOMA ICHINOSE
Photography

MARK E. JARRETT
Photo Art Direction

ROBERT PELUCE
Illustrations

WAYNE MASSARELLI
Make-up

JAMES REVA
Clothes Design

JON MAYER
Inspiration

Also thank you to
TARYN POWER,
MICHELLE PHILLIPS and
JORJANA KELLAWAY
for gracing these pages;

EDDYE KAUFLER and
EVELYN MAYER
for your eagle eyes in editing;

MELINDA BENIOFF
for your invaluable assistance;

ROGER BENIOFF
for your constant support;

and my staff
GEORGE, ELAINE, SARA, CILA
who have assisted me in this
and all my other projects.